A Nature Walk

Written and Edited, by Don G. Ford

This is expressly a work of Fiction in case you were unaware of that FACT.

The names, characters, places, and events, are all the work of author's over-active imagination. The guy hardly sleeps!

A goal I have in life is to return the Poem to its noble place among literatures best-read storytelling that will make sense the first time through. Poems should NEVER leave a person scratching their head in wonder. We have been duped in our society to believe that a good poem should tease our minds, and make us feel intellectually inferior to writers of the poetic lines.

Sorry, I'm not buying it, and I never have. You know things have gotten out of hand when people cringe when they hear a poet is going to do a reading. That is just criminal. The POEM should be a delight to read, to listen too, and to simply enjoy, making for a better day for everyone. The scratching of the head must stop. Most forms of writing in a book, magazine, or trade journal, should be understandable and not after reading the piece a dozen times.

"The POEM should be a delight to read, to listen too, and to simply enjoy…"

This DEDICATION goes out first and foremost to Andrew and Erin, my children and best story listeners.

If you enjoy the look, sound, and feel of nature, this book of poetry journeys was crafted especially for readers like you.

The young and those who are simply youthful at heart will enjoy these story-like poems.

PREFACE

I Feel I've Known You Always

An invitation carries me,

As I head out in the wood.

The air all crisp and clean;

The walk will do me good,

Sometimes I skip and kick a stone,
Or moving on I'll stop and stare.
I'll look hard at a squirrel's nest
To watch for any movement there.

I'll study how they did it,
Without the duct tape or the glue.
The wind will blow and not disturb,
And all that I recall is true.

I hear the blue jay just ahead.
He is the eyes and ears for all.
He leads the wildlife, so it's said;
And sometimes sounds his trouble call.

The deer is color blind, I'm told;
But not the turkey in the tree.
He spies our movements from above.
He keeps his eyes on you and me.

Another bird I chance did meet.
And what occurred you won't believe:
A bully crow and hummingbird.
Follow on this path with me.

He turned attention to his foe.
And you will see no fear showed he.
This hummingbird just drilled him through.
And to the ground, he fell near me.

Walking by a stream surprised me.
His tail was wide and flat I know.
I must have scared this other friend,
And pounding water, what a show.

I jumped out of my skin that day.
The beaver gave his warning call.
Torpedo-like, he moved in water.
"Do not intrude my space at all!"

I'll not forget this nature place.
I now know how I play a part.
My other home away from home,
And coming here I find my heart.

When writers try to fly their works, some of them fall down. But they must always flap their wings - to get off of the ground.

d.g.ford

Sound of Nature

From this nature place - I learned

To spread my wings. I learned

The forest songs – I heard

Them calling out my name.

I stood - I gazed in awe;

Its peaceful splendor too sublime

Its calm alluring draw

Of land, of water's shore and trees,

I've come to love this nature place,

It all keeps calling out to me

And though I claim it to be mine;

Its strength is in its beauty there.

Come and join me – come and dine.

It's here for all of us to share.

HOW A POEM FORMS

Mirror, mirror on the wall
Show the greatest poem of all
"Trees" of course without a doubt
That's what poems are all about

See Joyce Kilmer's "Trees" poem here *
It's shown below, have no fear
And if you've never read this one
So read it now, just for fun.

Now you'll see my commentary
Certain myths we can bury
Other thoughts I will unearth
Showing us their depth and worth

Poems are seen in candlelight
Things going bump in the night
Poems could rise from mundane acts
Pickles at night - as a snack

Setting of a dinner space
Every fork and spoon in place
Some see poems in canvass art
Or some in pie that's not too tart

Know how a poem comes to me?
List'ning to the rain - you see
Ev'ry sound and emotion
I see it like a magic potion

Can a poem fall from the sky?
This Chicken Little won't deny
A poem forms from anything
Listen for that special ring

A meter, rhyme, and its measure
Stir and mix it up for pleasure
Cook it up and when it's done
You must admit, poems are fun!

*Trees

BY JOYCE KILMER
I think that I shall never see
A poem lovely as a tree.

A tree whose hungry mouth is prest
Against the earth's sweet flowing breast;

A tree that looks at God all day,
And lifts her leafy arms to pray;

A tree that may in Summer wear
A nest of robins in her hair;

Upon whose bosom snow has lain;
Who intimately lives with rain.

Poems are made by fools like me,
But only God can make a tree.

Source: *Poetry* (August 1913).

Let the Wind Blow

The wind we see it, where it is

And where it goes at times

Rustling through the trees

Moving leaves and branches

And when the breeze stands still

You know it's simply waiting

To summon winds and gales

Becomes a mystery to most

You often feel a gentle brush

Upon cheek or through the hair

When the winds blow furiously

And trees bow, touch the ground

It garners awesome powers

Times astride with lightning

With thunder, rain, and the like

We know it's up to mischief

We see it topple over buildings

And taking trees right with it

Nothing in its path seems safe

So under shelter wise men go

When we think of gentle breezes

And their purpose on this earth

How the struggling butterflies

And bird on wing seem helpless

Without the wind to lift them up

And carry them in their flight

So come dear wind and blow

Upon the land - we welcome you

And if you must at times blow hard

We'll seek a shelter from the storm

The wind has its own moods that go from gentle to very outrageous. We have no control over it, and it sometimes overwhelms us. We just need to be prepared and find shelter when it's acting at its worst. In the end, all of life still needs the wind.

The End of Winter's Stay

(Two crows sat noiseless in a tree
Refused in silence to compete)
*

One morning when I had awoke
And stepped outside to join the day
Greeted by melodious sounds
The birds of fall returned today

These songbirds had arrived quite early
I'd better get a move on
And I was joining them of late
I still had missed their opening song

The chorus swelled as more joined in
Not one or two but dozens came
All I saw were crows of winter
All I heard were birds of spring

Though snow lie all around us
So convinced were they in song
They never stop their chanting
They rang their anthems strong

If words be put to all their notes
Calling for the warm sun rays
Melt away the cold long night
Of winters long enduring stay

So amidst this cloud white stuff
Lay spread as blankets all around
We're happy then to see it go
In silence melt into the ground

Listen well the chorus call
It's time for all the snow to go
The birds keep singing from the trees
It's time to view the flower show

The cold and dark of winter sleep
The bulbs of spring will start to climb
Their colors then will join in song
In mingled anthem so sublime

A royal time of new beginnings
The birds their songs had ushered in
We welcome spring with open arms
Up from the earth new life begins

All Noiseless in the Woods

The woods were very quiet today
Not a peep - not a word
Nor sound of squirrel chatter
Not a single bird was heard

A silence settled in all over
A quiet hush and gentle stillness
And then the silence it was broken
By a simple humble little cricket

The tune at first he played it softly
A click and then a tin, tin, tin
The blue jay then had joined the tune
Others too had joined right in

This day that started out in silence
Replaced by clanging, banging sounds
Too noisy for our little guy
Our cricket didn't stick around

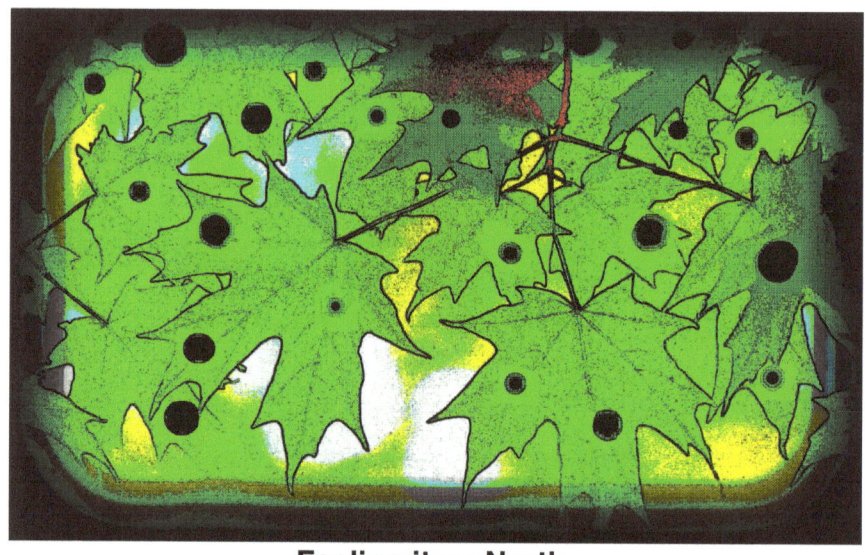

Feeling it up North

Here is a tree that feels the pain
It is shedding some oily tears
And it's showing up on its leaves
Awakening our many fears

Why is this problem coming North?
What did we do to merit this?
I see it as their own problem
Instead, they've left a dirty kiss

Will someone help us in our plight?
How can we remove this oil spot?
And save a tree from this cruel curse
Get here before the trees all rot

But like a lightning bolt it hit
It landed square upon my head

Forgot about our friends down South
Their birds and fish and trees all dead

There must be something we can do
Write some letters, raise awareness
It's time for all to show concern
Done nothing yet I must confess

Forgive me God, I didn't care
My fellow countrymen need me
I'll find a way to bring them help
I'll start the work upon my knee

Author Notes

I found these leaves all tar-spotted and saw a story piece unfolding- enjoy! It is not just a Southern problem or a regional disaster. The "Oil Spill" affects all Americans. We are one big United States and the situation in the Gulf region has come here too. We should all find a way to pitch in or lend a hand! As writers we know what to do.

Look for a book with my works regarding the Gulf Oil Spill Tragedy called "This Ones For the Birds" To order a copy and donate to the bird refuge :
http://www.wingsofhopenow.com/page2.html

Subject: **Poem published in October 2009**

The Shine Journal

Moonlit Nights

Overcasting dark the night

"I am the Moon in deadpan skies"

after splash of Sun : its light

reflected on what's down below

Every watcher feels the glow

if they could share a word

to open all the eyes and ears

it would simply be - welcome

The night is dark beyond all reason

coming there the lunar changes

moods and attitudes are altered

and warmly wanted is the light

The canopy now is overspread

spilling onto roofs and treetops

washing into windows won't

wake those asleep, adrift in dreams

This Moon, softly casting shadows

mixed emotions generate freely

with open thoughts and gazing up

we focus then such concentration

Skyward bound - eyes are fixed

but staying focused on the orb

They smile who look upon its faces

from right to top to side and end

another phase is seen tonight

every evening, a new tale's told

Moon's King, the Sun, is held

in highest reverence and in awe

a lowering of the head and heart

the Moon it knows its place above.

[Motivation: Abstract feeling that sheds light on the moon and its glow and position in the sky in the broader spectrum of thought.]

You see more than a picture, you hear the sounds

of the morning as it breaks.

A New Day Dawns

It rises on a dark horizon,

Lifting hope and expectation.

Dreams that otherwise might die,

It shines its light on all creation.

Shining bright beyond the veil;

Slowly drawing back the curtain.

All's not lost - the sun is up;

A new day dawns for certain.

Suddenly the heart it leaps,
Skips and frolics all about.
The tears of yesterday are gone,
All dried up and driven out.

Happy to see the sun come up,
The waking of a brand new day.
New times and places just ahead.
We must move on without delay.

For all the dreams in sleep we saw –
All the hopes we waited for,
The warm rays of a rising sun,
A better day - new open doors.

Close of Day Reflections

Across the calm clear waters,
To a sun-lit mirrored shore.
The brightness of the day is docking,
Reminders of what's gone before.

Before those shadows start to creep,
Before all daylight wanes,
You'll find me deep in all my thoughts -
My navigation to reclaim.

This last ditch effort by the sun
To leave a bright impression;
To shine a path of light for all,
To make its final declaration.

Once Gone - It's Gone Forever

Water cascades over the brink
Falling, spilling endlessly
No effort expended in the fall
Always leaving, not returning

Gone but followed on its heels
Behind itself more water comes
Continues on in moving cycles
Tumbling, rumbling sounds heard

Rising bubbles and foam churning
At the bottom briskly carried off
Can water run and last forever?
Will it always quench the thirst?

How we care for these cool waters
Well determines what's in store
Someday, soon, brooks are silent
Maybe no more streams and rivers

Gone the sound of water lapping
Will shorelines matter any more?
Can we shake the guilt and blame?
The waters can never return again.

Author Notes

This is a free verse poem that is not meant to rhyme.
Only time will tell how long before we use up this life
giving flow. There are efforts under way to conserve
this resource and to clean up the pollutants found in it.
But is there enough time left? We better all hope and
pray there is! It seems that time is never on our side.

SPECIAL Note: This arrived this morning. A lake near
us is being reclaimed and is starting to look pretty good.
This is great news, since this lake has been on the worst
water environmental list for some time.

A beautiful picture we paint with the first snow.
The Old Man

The blowing, gusty winds do come
Stubborn leaves now fall off trees
Branches then must brace themselves
Fall has long since taken leave

The frightful look of winter
He visits us all draped in snow
As the old man settles in
His coat, our covering, head to toe

It shrouds the once green landscape
In a blanket of pure white
Falls in silence all about
To the child it brings delight

This old man winter's visit
He overstays his welcome
We anxiously await the spring
He runs his course and then some

Dumping tons of snow and ice
He puts on quite a winter show
Holding fast his noble place
As we all chant: "It's time to go"

Author Notes
Picture the Old Man coming in all of his wintry garb.

Smiling Faces

I can't say I've ever met

A flower I didn't like

They come with smiles upon each face

Always they're a welcome sight

They add such color to our world

Taking turns they make us smile

It seems they're always very happy

Full of character and style.

Why can't we do as they do?

Live our lives in joyful play

They have their share of difficulties

Fighting hard to make their way

And yet they find the will to grow

Sometimes cold or drenched by rain

But they spring back so happily

Their composure they regain

In early spring up through the snow

Or up through the stubborn sod or clay

Take a tip from smiling faces

Just grin and have a better day.

Author Notes: Flowers have a unique way of looking at us, with that smile upon their faces. We only have to smile right back and then in a very small way we are able to commune with nature.

The last tree standing
My Tree and Me
Dedicated to other tree lovers

My Tree and Me

I heard a young child muse:
the human race will die for sure,
If all the trees are gone;
Without this air we won't endure.

The oxygen that they supply,
It won't return - it's gone.
The air we breathe is thinner now.
We can't survive for long.

Then all mankind will die.
We brought it on ourselves.
Expanding, building - leaving no trees.
by our pride and greed for wealth.

It left us poor and desolate.
One last tree - its life to give.
We tore it from its home - its soil,
Without regard its need to live.

Don G. Ford

This is storytelling throughout. If offers many paths for the traveler to go on. All are easy to read and make great bedtime adventures. If you are looking for amusement, this book will not disappoint you. New friends await you!

I WOKE UP FROM THIS DREAM

I looked outside my window pane,

A single tree was spotted there.

I ran and stood beside it,

So thankful for our air.

Instead of cutting down a tree,

I'll plant a thousand with my hands;

Replenishing more oxygen,

And spread this word across the land.

Notes: My daughter actually sparked this (story) poem. We were riding in the car and she gasped at a section of forest that was missing. In the Forestry business we call this a clear-cut. It is not a good practice, as it leaves many nearby trees vulnerable to the wind and weather - causing blow downs. "For a minute there Dad, I couldn't breathe," she said.

No Letting Go

I admire leaves I see on trees
That never let go - as you know
Hanging in midst Winter winds
Wild it blows, leaves on their toes

Determined are they to make my day
When other trees let go you see
Certain ones hold on for dear life
Through tons of snow - no letting go

To these the weather is never a bother
Something to say each and every day
So never give in if ya really wanna win
Our leaf never says - enough is enough

Hang in - stay strong - it may seem wrong
Chant "Greater is he that lives in thee"

Now make your aim to win this game
Let cold winds blow - put on their show

Thank a God above for his help and love
You are strong because God is along
You won't let go through winter snow
Then hang in tight and win this fight

Coming and Going

Hear the sound it makes;
As the rainbow it appears.
Its dazzling colors shout
All the sounds we think we hear.

Are joined by sighs of joy - relief
The rain it left - the sun it came
The 'bow' then melts away in silence
Its comings, goings - all the same.

TRAVELING SPRINGS

Splashes over rocks and walls

Crashing down, it speaks

It tells another nature tale

As water travels magically

It manages to thread its way

Among the outcrops, twisted, tossed

This rocky water bed is draped

In every color known to moss

The water constantly pours down

And travels as it washes through

As autumn adds a leafy sprinkle

Over rocks, runs free and cool

The water carries bushels full

Of fall's reminder - born on trees

Hauled away, it won't return

But calls for winter's cold and freeze

Now the water's name is ice

As crystals form a glaze

It covers like a frosting

Awaits the spring and warmer days

Oceans Alive

What difference could

d.g.ford

One life make?

The living breathing waters of the ocean
Rise and fall at no one's beckoning call
Above an ocean going vessel carves its path
Sails fill up of gusty breeze as gulls fly by

Below all manner of fish and aquatic life exist
These waters make a grand and giant home
Man may some day chose to live beneath
To surface only when he wants to view the sky

On top, within and down below, mysteries hide
Explorers plumb the depths of these deep seas
They search for valuables and all lost things
Never found on maps - X marks the spot

Behind the water form the walls of stone
The mountains stand there as a backdrop
Both are like a vast domain for us to ponder
Much is hidden in the rock and in the deepest sea

Gems formed inside the earth are precious
Pearls, hidden beneath the folds of silken softness
Land and water hold the answers below their surface
The looking and desiring must begin within the heart

This is another part of my Oceans Alive poetry series:

The Pearl Keepers

It lives upon the ocean floor
Open for business all the time
But when it closes up its mouth
It traps its food inside

A search for jewels under blankets
Hidden in its many folds
Hidden in this secret place
And over time it grows

It maybe pink – it maybe white
I've also seen this gem in black.
No matter what the color is
No shine or luster does it lack.

Another girl's best friend they say,
With shiny – softer glow
As bubbles rise from oyster shells
Not all have pearls in tow.

Early Winter Sounds

The tiny hammer inside of it fell
Which caused the clock to chime
The wind whistled past my ear
In my quiet solitary place today

My clock on the wall said 2 p.m.
As my afternoon was rushing by
Seems that evening brought it on
Fall had arrived and was in the air

Nothing gentle was in the breeze
Instead the howling of it heard
In search I was of peace of mind
Sitting warmly by my fireplace

The leaves all carried on the wind
Best to view them out the window
The hidden voice of Winter calling
Wrapped in the clothing of the Fall

Her Name is Iris
Background

These short stories, whether in poetry or prose, are the random musings on the merry-go-round of my mind. Some are real adventures in time; others are just fairy tales. You are welcome to come along with me on this nature trail and journey.

Iris has a tale to tell,
Her story will unfold.
A bold and elegant display,
Her colors, petals - we behold.

Perchance the sun is out today.
It adds some warmth, a smile.
Though Iris faces are short lived,
A grand appearance for a while.

And gazing we are carried off,
These mesmerizing flowers;
They know that they are being watched,
By each of us for untold hours.

Author Notes
**Their colors are too short lived. But their style and
hues, they amaze us just the same.**

Came Thunder and the Rain

Dedicated to Johnny Lewis my

cousin taken by lightning in 1963

The thunder warns us it is coming;

On its trail the lightning strikes.

It rumbles, slamming both fists down.

It's loud, persuasive, full of fight.

The face of children turning pale;

As each time it keeps crashing down.

Run and hide - but stay inside

Until the storm has made its rounds.

The rain will likely visit too;

As dark clouds suddenly let go.

And down in torrents from above;

It joins the storm - an awesome show.

It was an awful day. This day I will never forget, as we received the dreadful phone call. Johnny's been struck by lightning. He didn't survive.

My best friend and cousin, Johnny, was hit by lightning in 1963. Some things we will never let ourselves forget. Now that it's in a book, we never let others forget either.

See "Came Thunder and the Rain". This book is solely dedicated to Johnny Lewis, taken from us way too early at the age of 12. See it here >

https://www.createspace.com/4404633

The Sound of Rain Come Down

Background
These short stories, whether in poetry or prose, are the random musings on the merry-go-round of my mind. Some are real adventures in time; others are just fairy tales. You are welcome to come along with me on this nature trail and journey.

It starts as gentle footsteps.
The rain begins to fall.
Its rhythm and its beat -
Like whispers in the hall.

We can't quite make the words out.
Is it saying things at all?
I'm sure it's talking to me -
A word or two will fall.

I press my ear to panes of glass.
I want to know its secrets.
Then suddenly the sound gets loud,
The water falls without regret.

The words run all together;
Like a train that's chugging endlessly.
The new sounds I don't want to hear -
I think the rain is mad at me.

But then as quickly as it started,
The rain begins to quiet down.
I'm glad it stopped its yelling.
I'm glad it found its calm.

Heart Shaped Valentine Memories

By Don Ford

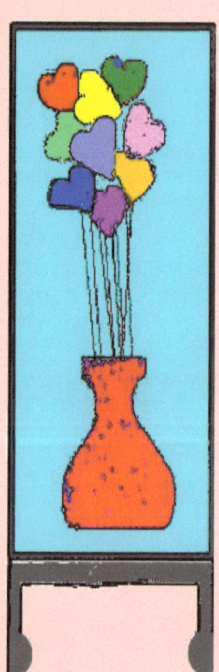

These Roses are hearts
These daisies are too
A vase full of blooms
Brought here for you.
You won't need to water
Or fuss with these flowers
Just enjoy all their colors
Through all daylight hours
Each heart is a memory
Of all we have done
Of times in the shadow
And great times in the sun

d.g.ford

The Tidal Wave

(Practicing my 5 minute poem)

The following short stories and poems are from my Oceans Alive series. Join me as we plumb the depths of the sea. We will go on adventures and meet new friends under the waves. Let's go and find out what's down there, so many leagues under the sea.

Oceans   Alive

So determined and destructive

Of frothy cold descending

Lifts itself and then it falls

Hits the shore ferociously

Comes in torrents like the rain

Leaving little in its wake

In nature - pounding and relentless

No way to hold it back at all

And nothing stands within its path

Angrily forcing its way through

Nothing calm or tranquil here

Frigid waters lend a hand

It leaves behind a devastation

With waves that billow o'er the land

When you build a fire. Let me restate that: When you get ready to build a fire, you must assemble all the necessary elements. Leaving out one ingredient, could be disastrous. LOL So it is with writing a personal poem. Ask the right questions about the subject you are writing about. Then carefully assemble them. Below is a poem I wrote about a dad, three young daughters, and the garden and flowers he loved. These he wanted all combined somehow. So see it below:

Dedicated to a dad with three daughters.

THREE FLOWERS IN MY GARDEN BLOOM

And in a Father's garden,
Three gentle flowers grow.
Their petals open wide:
Their faces we behold.

"My children," cries their Father.
"Stay safe within my garden wall.
May only gentle breezes blow;
My hope for you: Grow strong and tall.

And through the years stay close to me.
You'll always feel your Father's heart.
It ever reaches out to you,
Even if someday we part.

Remember this: your garden home,
In case you ever move away.
Your Father's never far from you;
In my heart three petals stay."

Author Notes: This was originally a request by a dad who loved his garden and his three girls. So I penned this for him. I signed this piece and put it in a frame, and it is on his office wall today. Smiles, Don

Leaves that Fall

(Autumn Haiku)

orange leaf descends

the Earth shouts out a welcome

final resting place

DON FORD ; AKA dgford, grassroots08, greywolf

Favorite Quote: "the best writing is rewriting" - E.B. White

Sometimes he is up typing or writing into the wee hours, until his fingers fall off. Now you know he writes fiction, but he also writes in every other genre. Poetry is a specialty of his and he likes to experiment.

Storytelling is his keynote and he's paid very well. Shares at retirement homes, schools, and churches. He has a strong faith in his Creator and knows that we are all stewards of this worlds' environmental resources.

What Do You Write?
Poetry, Fiction, Non Fiction, Children's, Play-writing, Other
How Many Years Have You Been Writing?
It all began at age 15, so quite a while.
Favorite Books and Authors
E. B. White (For the kid in me)
Western authors too numerous to list (For the Cowboy in me)
Robert Louis Stevenson, Frost and a host of others (For the Poet in me)
Hitchcock and H.G. Wells (Figure this one out yourself)

When I attended college art classes, I had no idea that at the end of the year my art instructor would request to keep my art.

Believe me when I say I never saw myself as some super artist; a simple artist maybe. I was just a student trying to tell a story with a picture.

Now that I have established myself as a published writer, andhave a few international pieces under my belt, I am combining my statement to join together my stories and my art. Most of my art is created from photos, of simple objects, and when completed have much to say. Some whisper a tale, while others like "My Blast From the Past" shouts a message.

Half of the battle for me in my art in particular is the choice of the right colors. Much of my writing and art combine to place the viewer and reader into the thick of the action. All of the work of writing and art has put me on a better road to success, which is not always about the monetary benefits. Cheers, Don

See a few art samples to follow. Many of mine are photos of real objects and I add some color and imagination.

www.ingramcontent.com/pod-product-compliance
Lightning Source LLC
Chambersburg PA
CBHW050821290526
45792CB00001B/209